P9-COO-812

'Art'

Yasmina Reza's first play, *Conversations après un Enterrement*, won her the Best Author Molière Award and the New Writer Award from the SACD in 1987. Her work for theatre and cinema includes *La Traversée de l'Hiver* and *L'Homme du Hasard* and a prize-winning adaptation of Stephen Berkoff's version of Kafka's *La Metamorphose*, and the screenplays *Jusqu'a la Nuit, Jim Mode Ne Pour Aider* and *A Demain*.

Christopher Hampton was born in the Azores in 1946. He wrote his first play, *When Did You Last See My Mother?*, at the age of eighteen. His work for the theatre, television and cinema includes *The Philanthropist*, adaptations from Ibsen and Molière and the screenplays *Dangerous Liaisons, Carrington* and *The Secret Agent*, the last two of which he also directed.

YASMINA REZA

'Art'

translated by
Christopher Hampton

ff

faber and faber
LONDON · BOSTON

First published in 1996
by Faber and Faber Limited
3 Queen Square London WC1N 3AU

Typeset by Faber and Faber Ltd
Printed in England by Mackays of Chatham plc, Chatham, Kent

ISBN 0-571-19014-6

Introduction

In the late Summer of 1996, I first heard about a play called '*Art.*' It arrived in London triumphantly after winning awards in France, and Yasmina Reza, the writer, was riding high with this piece that seemed to touch the heart of the relationship between three men. It is a play about friendship as much as one about Modern Art, contemporary morals, or the vagaries of consumerism. And with Christopher Hampton's name attached as the translator/adaptor, the enterprise gave off a heady, classy fragrance.

My agent wondered if I would be interested in coming back to London to do a new play in the West End. Was it an offer, I asked vainly? Well, no, not quite an offer, more like an approach to discover if I might be worth approaching. I was at the end of a continuous stint of work that had kept me away from home for the better part of the year. The timing was awful, so I said no without even reading the play. I just knew that one glance, one sniff of it, and I would lose my resolve. Just the "feel" of a play can do that to an actor, so I kept a safe distance away. And yet, despite my best intentions, something inside me was unwilling to sever my contact with the play quite so soon. I sent a message to David Pugh, the producer, that if an American production was ever in the cards, I would love to be considered. I'm not sure that I took the possibility of doing the play on Broadway very seriously. Actors are the first to assume that someone else will get the role as a form of self-defense in the event someone else actually does.

I found myself in London later in the year and, by this time, the show had opened to fantastic reviews. The kind you would be embarrassed to write for yourself. The cast was starry with Albert Finney, Tom Courteney and Ken Stott, who, although less well-known than the others, was walking away with the laurels. Ken was playing Ivan. A bell went off in my head. Wasn't that the role mentioned to me all those months ago? Perhaps I should have read the sodding thing after all. Sitting in a coffee bar somewhere in SoHo, I began to consider how feasible doing the play in New York was. There was no talk of it, but a hit is a hit, and hits can swim the Atlantic. I live in the States, they know that; I have my Green Card and I'm eligible to work on Broadway, blah, blah, blah. So went my private reverie, growing more hysterical by the second. Each sip of my espresso fuelling my fantasy. I saw myself in a rehearsal room in Manhattan, reducing my colleagues to delirious tears with my anecdotes, each one more rib-cracking than the last; in my dressing room backstage, drowning in flowers. Then, magically, on a podium, making my acceptance speech. This had to stop. Looking out of the coffee-shop window, I saw a taxi driver getting upset with a delivery truck blocking his way. A few threats were exchanged, and fists were shook. I tried to recapture the world that had been in my mind a few moments before. I was shaming myself. I hadn't even seen the production in London, let alone read the play. I decided to do both.

The play, according to the general lean of the critics, was a crowd-pleaser. The central theme is accessible enough. Modern Art, in the realm of public opinion, is an easy target. In the play, Marc, one of the friends, becomes a kind of spokesman for the audience. Pretention, or the suspicion of it, is always good for a laugh, and that particular seam is a rich one in this play. One of the less kind reviews suggested the play was a lightweight piece masquerading as a major work. After seeing it twice with two different casts, and reading it several times, I'm convinced it is a masterpiece posing as a Boulevard romp. I knew I had to do this play, but I feared I'd missed my chance. I'd said no for the best reason in the world. My work was keeping me away from my family for too long. I needed to be at home. All these feelings were true and valid, but deep down, in the part of me where my ego runs free, I was kicking myself. New York had to be mine. I was shocked at my willingness to discard my good intentions for the opportunity of doing a play on Broadway. I was not known for this kind of naked, driven behavior. Or was I?

Christmas 1996. Back in Los Angeles, exhausted from a year of constant working. It is ironic, and somewhat dangerous, when actors moan about working too much. I mention it with care, but I truly was dog-tired. There was no need to worry because that winter ushered in the longest stretch of unemployment I'd had to endure in years. As if in response to my smug, self-satisfied complaints about working too much, my job prospects went south. It felt like I was being picked up and turned upside down and shaken until the change fell out of my pockets. Every audition, interview and meeting I went to had the lustre of old fish. A smell was coming off me. That needy smell when you enter a room with no confidence, and then leave with barely your self-loathing in one piece. Into this creative desert came word that *Art* was possibly on its way to New York, and I was being considered. Still not an offer. Word was that Sean Connery, the other producer, was looking for a stellar cast that would turn this transfer into the Theatrical Event of the year. The show was on its second cast in London, still playing to full houses and garnering even more superlative reviews than the first. This play wasn't just a theatrical event, it had become Olympian. In May '97, I was flown to New York to meet David Pugh and Joan Cullman and to have a session with Matthew Warchus, who was to repeat his directing duties in New York. This was a big-time meeting, the tension relaxed a little by the fact that David and I have known each other since the days when neither of us had done much worth talking about. My friendship with him was my only ace. No one else involved knew me from Adam. The meeting was to be held at Joan Cullman's East Side penthouse apartment. I use the word "apartment" purely for convenience. This inner-city palace took my breath away. Two floors, both, I think, with wraparound terraces that put you above the city with views all around, views you only see in movies about people who own these kinds of places. I was dumbstruck. David and his party were late so Joan and I (may I call you Joan?) sat and talked for an hour. I suddenly thought, 'This is part of the meeting, she wants to give me the once-over on her own. Why not? She's putting up a truckload of money, after all.' Joan is married to Mr. Cullman, who is a huge noise with one of the big tobacco companies. I figured it must okay to smoke, so I lit up hoping to God I hadn't chosen a rival brand. Joan declined one of mine, preferring to keep her habit within the family. She kept up a narrative about some of the fabulous artwork on the walls, including a Wyeth. While she talked, she was opening drawers looking for her fags. There were cartons everywhere. Suddenly, packets of snout were popping up wherever my eyes came to rest. I wondered if the old man ever chided her for helping herself to the stock. The hour flew by, aided by nicotine and generous amounts of very good Malt Whisky. I was feeling right at home when David and the others arrived. David apologised courteously, letting us know who had the status at that moment. More drink appeared, more cigarettes, the talk got chattier and more camp. Joan, who had been a charming hostess throughout, now revealed an appealing sense of humour as well as a comprehensive knowledge of Theatre. She was no newcomer to throwing her cash at the money pit known as the Great White Way.

After some more drink, Matthew Warchus and I went upstairs to a room designed with peacocks on the wall to discuss in private our concerns and desires as far as doing *Art* together. I was already convinced the part was mine. Then Matthew confused me with talk of a different role then that I had always thought of. He wondered if I might consider Marc, the role Albert Finney had played. I was delighted, but still confused. He had another surprise in store and that was the idea of three actors rotating all three roles. I was afire with excitement. The booze and free smokes had kicked in and I was as high as a kite. I looked out of the window to the view across the city and I remember the first thought in my head was of my mother, dressed in her fake fur and cultured pearls, trotting into a dressing room with me at the mirror taking off makeup after a show. She always wore the same outfit and invariably said the same thing: "Fredo, this is the best show I see you do. I so proud of you, Fredo!" Regardless of the quality, or otherwise, of what she saw me in, the reaction from her was never less than ecstatic. She died before I had really gotten anywhere and, even now, when something delicious happens, I think of how she would be enjoying it. Sitting next to me with her favorite tipple, a sweet vermouth over ice, telling whoever stopped long enough to listen how she always knew her Fredo was destined for wonderful things. She loved me being an actor. One of the joys of my working life was introducing her to friends and colleagues, who would fall for her Italian accent and her flirtatiousness. As I gazed into the New York sky, now beginning to darken, my mother's face receded and I was dragged back to the present by Matthew's voice as he explained some ideas he had for casting. I was drunk and had stopped listening, to be honest. I suspect he noticed, as it was he who suggested we join the others for our supper. The whole evening was dreamlike after that. I ate like a fool and talked far too much. I even managed to make a slight exhibition of myself with Joan Cullman's maid. I noticed her Latin accent and I guessed Central America, so, in Spanish, I asked where she was from. My grasp of my father's native tongue is clearly better when I am sober because I messed up my tenses or some such thing. I must have done alright because when I asked her, she gazed at me in mild surprise and replied, "The kitchen, *señor*."

Characters

Marc
Serge
Yvan

The main room of a flat.
　　A single set. As stripped-down and neutral as possible.
　　The scenes unfold, successively, at Serge's, Yvan's and Marc's.
　　Nothing changes, except for the painting on the wall.

'Art' received its British première in this translation at Wyndhams Theatre, London, on 15 October 1996. The cast was as follows:

Marc Albert Finney
Serge Tom Courtenay
Yvan Ken Stott

Directed by Matthew Warchus
Designed by Mark Thompson
Lighting by Hugh Vanstone
Music by Gary Yershon
Produced by David Pugh and Sean Connery

Marc, alone.

Marc My friend Serge has bought a painting. It's a canvas about five foot by four: white. The background is white and if you screw up your eyes, you can make out some fine white diagonal lines.

Serge is one of my oldest friends.

He's done very well for himself, he's a dermatologist and he's keen on *art*.

On Monday, I went to see the painting; Serge had actually got hold of it on the Saturday, but he'd been lusting after it for several months.

This white painting with white lines.

At Serge's.

At floor level, a white canvas with fine white diagonal scars. Serge looks at his painting, thrilled. Marc looks at the painting. Serge looks at Marc looking at the painting.

Long silence: from both of them, a whole range of wordless emotions.

Marc Expensive?

Serge Two hundred thousand.

Marc Two hundred thousand?

Serge Huntingdon would take it off my hands for two hundred and twenty.

Marc Who's that?

Serge Huntingdon?

Marc Never heard of him.

Serge Huntingdon! The Huntingdon Gallery!

Marc The Huntingdon Gallery would take it off your hands for two hundred and twenty?

Serge No, not the Gallery. Him. Huntingdon himself. For his own collection.

Marc Then why didn't Huntingdon buy it?

Serge It's important for them to sell to private clients. That's how the market circulates.

Marc Mm hm . . .

Serge Well?

Marc . . .

Serge You're not in the right place. Look at it from this angle.
Can you see the lines?

Marc What's the name of the . . .?

Serge Painter. Antrios.

Marc Well-known?

Serge Very. Very!

Pause.

Marc Serge, you haven't bought this painting for two hundred thousand francs?

Serge You don't understand, that's what it costs. It's an Antrios.

Marc You haven't bought this painting for two hundred thousand francs?

Serge I might have known you'd miss the point.

Marc You paid two hundred thousand francs for this shit?

Serge, as if alone.

Serge My friend Marc's an intelligent enough fellow, I've always valued our relationship, he has a good job, he's an aeronautical engineer, but he's one of those new-style intellectuals, who are not only enemies of modernism, but seem to take some sort of incomprehensible pride in running it down . . .

In recent years these nostalgia-merchants have become quite breathtakingly arrogant.

Same pair. Same place. Same painting.
  Pause.

Serge What do you mean, 'this shit'?

Marc Serge, where's your sense of humour? Why aren't you laughing? . . . It's fantastic, you buying this painting.

  Marc laughs. Serge remains stony.

Serge I don't care how fantastic you think it is, I don't mind if you laugh, but I would like to know what you mean by 'this shit'.

Marc You're taking the piss!

Serge No, I'm not. By whose standards is it shit? If you call something shit, you need to have some criterion to judge it by.

Marc Who are you talking to? Who do you think you're talking to? Hello! . . .

Serge You have no interest whatsoever in contemporary painting, you never have had. This is a field about which you know absolutely nothing, so how can you assert that any given object, which conforms to laws you don't understand, is shit?

Marc Because it is. It's shit. I'm sorry.

Serge, alone.

Serge He doesn't like the painting.
Fine . . .
But there was no warmth in the way he reacted.
No attempt.
No warmth when he dismissed it out of hand.
Just that vile, pretentious laugh.
A real know-all laugh.
I hated that laugh.

Marc, alone.

Marc It's a complete mystery to me, Serge buying this painting. It's unsettled me, it's filled me with some indefinable unease.
When I left his place, I had to take three capsules of Gelsemium 9X which Paula recommended – Gelsemium or Ignatia, she said, Gelsemium or Ignatia, which do you prefer, I mean, how the hell should I know? – because I couldn't begin to understand how Serge, my friend, could have bought that picture.
Two hundred thousand francs!
He's comfortably off, but he's hardly rolling in money.
Comfortable, no more, just comfortable. And he spends two hundred grand on a white painting.
I must go and see Yvan, he's a friend of ours, I have to

discuss this with Yvan. Mind you, Yvan's a very tolerant bloke, which of course, when it comes to relationships, is the worst thing you can be.

Yvan's very tolerant because he couldn't care less.

If Yvan tolerates the fact that Serge has spent two hundred grand on some piece of white shit, it's because he couldn't care less Serge.

Obviously.

At Yvan's.
On the wall, some daub.
Yvan is on all fours with his back to us. He seems to be looking for something underneath a piece of furniture. As he does so, he turns to introduce himself.

Yvan I'm Yvan.

I'm a bit tense at the moment, because, having spent my life in textiles, I've just found a new job as a sales agent for a wholesale stationery business.

People like me. My professional life has always been a failure and I'm getting married in a couple of weeks. She's a lovely intelligent girl from a good family.

Marc enters. Yvan has resumed his search and has his back to him.

Marc What are you doing?

Yvan I'm looking for the top of my pen.

Time passes.

Marc All right, that's enough.

Yvan I had it five minutes ago.

Marc It doesn't matter.

Yvan Yes, it does.

Marc gets down on his knees to help him look. Both of them spend some time looking. Marc straightens up.

Marc Stop it. Buy another one.

Yvan It's a felt-tip, they're special, they'll write on any surface . . . It's just infuriating. Objects, I can't tell you how much they infuriate me. I had it in my hand five minutes ago.

Marc Are you going to live here?

Yvan Do you think it's suitable for a young couple?

Marc Young couple! Ha, ha . . .

Yvan Try not to laugh like that in front of Catherine.

Marc How's the stationery business?

Yvan All right. I'm learning.

Marc You've lost weight.

Yvan A bit. I'm pissed off about that top. It'll all dry up. Sit down.

Marc If you go on looking for that top, I'm leaving.

Yvan OK, I'll stop. You want something to drink?

Marc A Perrier, if you have one.
Have you seen Serge lately?

Yvan No. Have you?

Marc Yesterday.

Yvan Is he well?

Marc Very.
He's just bought a painting.

Yvan Oh yes?

Marc Mm.

Yvan Nice?

Marc White.

Yvan White?

Marc White.
   Imagine a canvas about five foot by four . . . with a white background . . . completely white in fact . . . with fine white diagonal stripes . . . you know . . . and maybe another horizontal white line, towards the bottom . . .

Yvan How can you see them?

Marc What?

Yvan These white lines. If the background's white, how can you see the lines?

Marc You just do. Because I suppose the lines are slightly grey, or vice versa, or anyway there are degrees of white! There's more than one kind of white!

Yvan Don't get upset. Why are you getting upset?

Marc You immediately start quibbling. Why can't you let me finish?

Yvan All right. Go on.

Marc Right. So, you have an idea of what the painting looks like.

Yvan I think so, yes.

Marc Now you have to guess how much Serge paid for it.

Yvan Who's the painter?

Marc Antrios. Have you heard of him?

Yvan No. Is he fashionable?

Marc I knew you were going to ask me that!

Yvan Well, it's logical . . .

Marc No, it isn't logical . . .

Yvan Of course it's logical, you ask me to guess the price, you know very well the price depends on how fashionable the painter might be . . .

Marc I'm not asking you to apply a whole set of critical standards, I'm not asking you for a professional valuation, I'm asking you what you, Yvan, would give for a white painting tarted up with a few off-white stripes.

Yvan Bugger all.

Marc Right. And what about Serge? Pick a figure at random.

Yvan Ten thousand francs.

Marc Ha!

Yvan Fifty thousand.

Marc Ha!

Yvan A hundred thousand.

Marc Keep going.

Yvan A hundred and fifty? Two hundred?!

Marc Two hundred. Two hundred grand.

Yvan No!

Marc Yes.

Yvan Two hundred grand?

Marc Two hundred grand.

Yvan Has he gone crazy?

Marc Looks like it.

Slight pause.

Yvan All the same . . .

Marc What do you mean, all the same?

Yvan If it makes him happy . . . he can afford it . . .

Marc So that's what you think, is it?

Yvan Why? What do you think?

Marc You don't understand the seriousness of this, do you?

Yvan Er . . . no.

Marc It's strange how you're missing the basic point of this story. All you can see is externals. You don't understand the seriousness of it.

Yvan What is the seriousness of it?

Marc Don't you understand what this means?

Yvan Would you like a cashew nut?

Marc Don't you see that suddenly, in some grotesque way, Serge fancies himself as a 'collector'.

Yvan Well . . .

Marc From now on, our friend Serge is one of the great connoisseurs.

Yvan Bollocks.

Marc Well of course it's bollocks. You can't buy your way in that cheap. But that's what *he* thinks.

Yvan Oh, I see.

Marc Doesn't that upset you?

Yvan No. Not if it makes him happy.

Marc If it makes him happy. What's that supposed to mean?

What sort of a philosophy is that, if it makes him happy?

Yvan As long as it's not doing any harm to anyone else . . .

Marc But it is. It's doing harm to me! I'm disturbed, I'm disturbed, more than that, I'm hurt, yes, I am, I'm fond of Serge, and to see him let himself be ripped off and lose every ounce of discernment through sheer snobbery . . .

Yvan I don't know why you're so surprised. He's always haunted galleries in the most absurd way, he's always been an exhibition freak.

Marc He's always been a freak, but a freak with a sense of humour. You see, basically, what really upsets me is that you can't have a laugh with him any more.

Yvan I'm sure you can.

Marc You can't!

Yvan Have you tried?

Marc Of course I've tried. I laughed. Heartily. What do you think I did? He didn't crack a smile.

Mind you, two hundred grand, I suppose it might be hard to see the funny side.

Yvan Yes.

They laugh.

I'll make him laugh.

Marc I'd be amazed. Any more nuts?

Yvan He'll laugh, you just wait.

At Serge's.
Serge is with Yvan. The painting isn't there.

Serge . . . and you get on with the in-laws?

Yvan Wonderfully. As far as they're concerned, I'm some berk tottering from one dodgy job to another and now I'm groping my way into the world of vellum . . . This thing on my hand, what is it?

Serge examines it.

Is it serious?

Serge No.

Yvan Oh, good. How are things?

Serge Nothing. Lot of work. Exhausted.
It's nice to see you. You never phone.

Yvan I don't like to disturb you.

Serge You're joking. You just speak to my secretary and I'll call you back right away.

Yvan I suppose so.
Your place gets more and more monastic . . .

Serge laughs.

Serge Yes!
Seen Marc recently?

Yvan Not recently, no.
Have you?

Serge Two or three days ago.

Yvan Is he all right?

Serge Yes. More or less.

Yvan Oh?

Serge No, he's all right.

Yvan I talked to him on the phone last week, he seemed all right.

Serge Well, he is. He's all right.

Yvan You seemed to be implying he wasn't all right.

Serge On the contrary, I said, he was all right.

Yvan More or less, you said.

Serge Yes, more or less. More or less all right.

Long silence. Yvan wanders around the room.

Yvan You been out? Seen anything?

Serge No. I can't afford to go out.

Yvan Oh?

Serge (*cheerfully*) I'm ruined.

Yvan Oh?

Serge You want to see something special? Would you like to?

Yvan Of course I would. Show me.

Serge exits and returns with the Antrios, which he turns round and sets down in front of Yvan.
Yvan looks at the painting and, strangely enough, doesn't manage the hearty laugh he'd predicted.
A long pause, while Yvan studies the painting and Serge studies Yvan.

Oh, yes. Yes, yes.

Serge Antrios.

Yvan Yes, yes.

Serge It's a seventies Antrios. Worth mentioning. He's going through a similar phase now, but this one's from the seventies.

Yvan Yes, yes.
 Expensive?

Serge In absolute terms, yes. In fact, no.
 You like it?

Yvan Oh, yes, yes, yes.

Serge Plain.

Yvan Plain, yes . . . Yes . . . And at the same time . . .

Serge Magnetic.

Yvan Mm . . . yes . . .

Serge You don't really get the resonance just at the moment.

Yvan Well, a bit . . .

Serge No, you don't. You have to come back in the middle of the day. That resonance you get from something monochromatic, it doesn't really happen under artificial light.

Yvan Mm hm.

Serge Not that it is actually monochromatic.

Yvan No! . . .
 How much was it?

Serge Two hundred thousand.

Yvan Very reasonable.

Serge Very.

Silence. Suddenly Serge bursts out laughing, immediately followed by Yvan. Both of them roar with laughter.

Crazy, or what?

Yvan Crazy!

Serge Two hundred grand!

Hearty laughter. They stop. They look at each other. They start again. Then stop.
They've calmed down.

Serge You know Marc's seen this painting.

Yvan Oh?

Serge Devastated.

Yvan Oh?

Serge He told me it was shit. A completely inappropriate description.

Yvan Absolutely.

Serge You can't call this shit.

Yvan No.

Serge You can say, I don't get it, I can't grasp it, you can't say 'it's shit'.

Yvan You've seen his place.

Serge Nothing to see.
   It's like yours, it's . . . what I mean is, you couldn't care less.

Yvan His taste is classical, he likes things classical, what do you expect . . .

Serge He started in with this sardonic laugh . . . Not a trace of charm . . . Not a trace of humour.

Yvan You know Marc is moody, there's nothing new about that . . .

Serge He has no sense of humour. With you, I can laugh. With him, I'm like a block of ice.

Yvan It's true he's a bit gloomy at the moment.

Serge I don't blame him for not responding to this painting, he hasn't the training, there's a whole apprenticeship you have to go through, which he hasn't, either because he's never wanted to or because he has no particular instinct for it, none of that matters, no, what I blame him for is his tone of voice, his complacency, his tactlessness.

I blame him for his insensitivity. I don't blame him for not being interested in modern Art, I couldn't give a toss about that, I like him for other reasons . . .

Yvan And he likes you!

Serge No, no, no, no, I felt it the other day, a kind of . . . a kind of condescension . . . contempt with a really bitter edge . . .

Yvan No, surely not!

Serge Oh, yes! Don't keep trying to smooth things over. Where d'you get this urge to be the great reconciler of the human race? Why don't you admit that Marc is atrophying? If he hasn't already atrophied.

Silence.

At Marc's.
  On the wall, a figurative painting: a landscape seen through a window.

Yvan We had a laugh.

Marc You had a laugh?

Yvan We had a laugh. Both of us. We had a laugh. I promise you on Catherine's life, we had a good laugh, both of us, together.

Marc You told him it was shit and you had a good laugh.

Yvan No, I didn't tell him it was shit, we laughed spontaneously.

Marc You arrived, you looked at the painting and you laughed. And then he laughed.

Yvan Yes. If you like. We talked a bit, then it was more or less as you described.

Marc A genuine laugh, was it?

Yvan Perfectly genuine.

Marc Well, then, I've made a mistake. Good. I'm really pleased to hear it.

Yvan It was even better than you think. It was Serge who laughed first.

Marc It was Serge who laughed first . . .

Yvan Yes.

Marc He laughed first and you joined in.

Yvan Yes.

Marc But what made him laugh?

Yvan He laughed because he sensed I was about to laugh. If you like, he laughed to put me at my ease.

Marc It doesn't count if he laughed first.
If he laughed first, it was to defuse your laughter.
It means it wasn't a genuine laugh.

Yvan It was a genuine laugh.

Marc It may have been a genuine laugh, but it wasn't for the right reason.

Yvan What is the right reason? I'm confused.

Marc He wasn't laughing because his painting is ridiculous, you and he weren't laughing for the same reasons, you were laughing at the painting and he was laughing to ingratiate himself, to put himself on your wavelength, to show you that on top of being an aesthete who can spend more on a painting than you earn in a year, he's still your same old subversive mate who likes a good laugh.

Yvan Mm hm . . .

A brief silence.

You know . . .

Marc Yes . . .

Yvan This is going to amaze you . . .

Marc Go on . . .

Yvan I didn't like the painting . . . but I didn't actually hate it.

Marc Well, of course. You can't hate what's invisible, you can't hate nothing.

Yvan No, no, it has something . . .

Marc What do you mean?

Yvan It has something. It's not nothing.

Marc You're joking.

Yvan I'm not as harsh as you. It's a work of art, there's a system behind it.

Marc A system?

Yvan A system.

Marc What system?

Yvan It's the completion of a journey . . .

Marc Ha, ha, ha!

Yvan It wasn't painted by accident, it's a work of art which stakes its claim as part of a trajectory . . .

Marc Ha, ha, ha!

Yvan All right, laugh.

Marc You're parroting out all Serge's nonsense. From him, it's heart-breaking, from you it's just comical!

Yvan You know, Marc, this complacency, you want to watch out for it. You're getting bitter, it's not very attractive.

Marc Good. The older I get, the more offensive I hope to become.

Yvan Great.

Marc A system!

Yvan You're impossible to talk to.

Marc There's a system behind it! . . . You look at this piece of shit, but never mind, never mind, there's a system behind it! . . . You reckon there's a system behind this landscape? (*He indicates the painting on his wall.*) . . . No, uh? Too evocative. Too expressive. Everything's on the canvas! No scope for a system! . . .

Yvan I'm glad you're enjoying yourself.

Marc Yvan, look, speak for yourself. Describe your feelings to me.

Yvan I felt a resonance.

Marc You felt a resonance? . . .

Yvan You're denying that I'm capable of appreciating this painting on my own account.

Marc Of course I am.

Yvan Well, why?

Marc Because I know you. Because apart from your disastrous indulgence, you're quite sane.

Yvan I wish I could say the same for you.

Marc Yvan, look me in the eye.

Yvan I'm looking at you.

Marc Were you moved by Serge's painting?

Yvan No.

Marc Answer me this. You're getting married tomorrow and you and Catherine get this painting as a wedding present. Does it make you happy? . . .
  Does it make you happy? . . .

Yvan, alone.

Yvan Of course it doesn't make me happy.
  It doesn't make me happy, but, generally speaking, I'm not the sort of person who can say I'm happy, just like that.
  I'm trying to . . . I'm trying to think of an occasion when I could have said yes, I'm happy . . . Are you happy to be getting married, my mother stupidly asked me one day, are you at least happy to be getting married? . . . Why wouldn't I be, mother?
  What do you mean, why wouldn't I be? You're either

happy or you're not happy, what's why wouldn't I be got to do with it? . . .

Serge, alone.

Serge As far as I'm concerned, it's not white.

When I say as far as I'm concerned, I mean objectively.

Objectively speaking, it's not white.

It has a white background, with a whole range of greys . . .

There's even some red in it.

You could say it's very pale.

I wouldn't like it if it was white.

Marc thinks it's white . . . that's his limit . . .

Marc thinks it's white because he's got hung up on the idea that it's white.

Unlike Yvan. Yvan can see it isn't white.

Marc can think what he likes, what do I care?

Marc, alone.

Marc Obviously I should have taken the Ignatia.

Why do I have to be so categorical?

What possible difference can it make to me, if Serge lets himself be taken in by modern Art?

I mean, it is a serious matter. But I could have found some other way to put it to him.

I could have taken a less aggressive tone.

Even if it makes me physically ill that my best friend has bought a white painting, all the same I ought to avoid attacking him about it.

I ought to be nice to him.

From now on, I'm on my best behaviour.

At Serge's.

Serge Feel like a laugh?

Marc Go on.

Serge Yvan liked the Antrios.

Marc Where is it? . . .

Serge You want another look?

Marc Fetch it out.

Serge I knew you'd come round to it! . . .

He exits and returns with the painting. A moment of contemplation.

Yvan got the hang of it. Right away.

Marc Mm.

Serge All right, listen, it's just a picture, we don't have to get bogged down with it, life's too short . . . By the way, have you read this? (*He picks up* De Vita Beata *by Seneca and throws it on to the low table just in front of Marc.*) Read it, it's a masterpiece.

Marc picks up the book, opens it and leafs through it.

Incredibly modern. Read that, you don't need to read anything else. What with the office, the hospital, Françoise, who's now decreed that I'm to see the children every weekend – which is something new for Françoise, the notion that children need a father – I don't have time to read any more, I'm obliged to go straight for the essentials.

Marc . . . As in painting . . . Where you've ingeniously eliminated form and colour. Those old chestnuts.

Serge Yes . . . Although I'm still capable of appreciating more figurative work. Like your Flemish job. Very restful.

Marc What's Flemish about it? It's a view of Carcassonne.

Serge Yes, but I mean . . . it's slightly Flemish in style . . . the window, the view, the . . . in any case, it's very pretty.

Marc It's not worth anything, you know that.

Serge What difference does that make? . . . Anyway, in a few years God knows if the Antrios will be worth anything! . . .

Marc . . . You know, I've been thinking. I've been thinking and I've changed my mind. The other day, driving across Paris, I was thinking about you and I said to myself: isn't there, deep down, something really poetic about what Serge has done? . . . Isn't surrendering to this incoherent urge to buy in fact an authentically poetic impulse?

Serge You're very conciliatory today. Unrecognizable. What's this bland, submissive tone of voice? It doesn't suit you at all, by the way.

Marc No, no, I'm trying to explain, I'm apologizing.

Serge Apologizing? What for?

Marc I'm too thin-skinned, I'm too highly strung, I overreact . . . You could say, I lack judgement.

Serge Read Seneca.

Marc That's it. See, for instance, you say 'read Seneca' and I could easily have got annoyed. I'm quite capable of being really annoyed by your saying to me, in the course of our conversation, 'read Seneca'. Which is absurd!

Serge No. It's not absurd.

Marc Really?

Serge No, because you thought you could identify . . .

Marc I didn't say I *was* annoyed . . .

Serge You said you could easily . . .

Marc Yes, yes. I could easily . . .

Serge Get annoyed, and I understand that. Because when I said 'read Seneca', you thought you could identify a kind of superiority. You tell me you lack judgement and my answer is 'read Seneca', well, it's obnoxious!

Marc It is, rather.

Serge Having said that, it's true you lack judgement, because I didn't say 'read Seneca', I said 'read Seneca!'

Marc You're right. You're right.

Serge The fact of the matter is, you've quite simply lost your sense of humour.

Marc Probably.

Serge You've lost your sense of humour, Marc. You really have lost your sense of humour, old chap. When I was talking to Yvan the other day, we agreed you'd lost your sense of humour. Where the hell is he? He's incapable of being on time, it's infuriating! We'll miss the beginning!

Marc . . . Yvan thinks I've lost my sense of humour? . . .

Serge Yvan agrees with me that recently you've somewhat lost your sense of humour.

Marc The last time you saw each other, Yvan said he liked your painting very much and I'd lost my sense of humour . . .

Serge Oh, yes, that, yes, the painting, really, very much. And he meant it . . . What's that you're eating?

Marc Ignatia.

Serge Oh, you believe in homeopathy now?

Marc I don't believe in anything.

Serge Didn't you think Yvan had lost a lot of weight?

Marc So's she.

Serge It's the wedding, eating away at them.

Marc Yes.

They laugh.

Serge How's Paula?

Marc All right. (*He indicates the Antrios.*) Where are you going to put it?

Serge Haven't decided. There. Or there? . . . Too ostentatious.

Marc Are you going to have it framed?

Serge laughs discreetly.

Serge No! . . . No, no . . .

Marc Why not?

Serge It's not supposed to be framed.

Marc Is that right?

Serge The artist doesn't want it to be. It mustn't be interrupted. It's already in its setting. (*He signals Marc over to examine the edge.*) Look . . . you see . . .

Marc What is it, Elastoplast?

Serge No, it's a kind of Kraft paper . . . Made up by the artist.

Marc It's funny the way you say the artist.

Serge What else am I supposed to say?

Marc You say the artist when you could say the painter or . . . whatever his name is . . . Antrios . . .

Serge So? . . .

Marc But you say the artist, as if he's a sort of . . . well, anyway, doesn't matter. What are we seeing? Let's try and see something with a bit of substance for once.

Serge It's eight o'clock. Everything will have started. I can't imagine how this man, who has nothing whatsoever to do – am I right? – manages to be late every single time. Where the fuck is he?

Marc Let's just have dinner.

Serge All right. It's five past eight. We said we'd meet between seven and half-past . . . What d'you mean, the way I say the artist?

Marc Nothing. I was going to say something stupid.

Serge Well, go on.

Marc You say the artist as if . . . as if he's some unattainable being. The artist . . . some sort of god . . .

 Serge laughs.

Serge Well, for me, he is a god! You don't think I'd have forked out a fortune for a mere mortal! . . .

Marc I see.

Serge I went to the Pompidou on Monday, you know how many Antrioses they have at the Pompidou? . . . Three! Three Antrioses! . . . At the Pompidou!

Marc Amazing.

Serge And mine's as good as any of them! If not better! . . .

25

Listen, I have a suggestion, let's give Yvan exactly three more minutes and then bugger off. I've found a very good new place. Lyonnaise.

Marc Why are you so jumpy?

Serge I'm not jumpy.

Marc Yes, you are jumpy.

Serge I am not jumpy, well, I am, I'm jumpy because this slackness is intolerable, this inability to practise any kind of self-discipline!

Marc The fact is, I'm getting on your nerves and you're taking it out on poor Yvan.

Serge What do you mean, poor Yvan, are you taking the piss? You're not getting on my nerves, why should you be getting on my nerves?

Serge He is getting on my nerves. It's true.
He's getting on my nerves.
It's this ingratiating tone of voice. A little smile behind every word.
It's as if he's forcing himself to be pleasant.
Don't be pleasant, whatever you do, don't be pleasant!
Could it be buying the Antrios? . . . Could buying the Antrios have triggered off this feeling of constraint between us?
Buying something . . . without his backing? . . .
Well, bugger his backing! Bugger your backing, Marc!

Marc Could it be the Antrios, buying the Antrios?
No –
It started some time ago . . .
To be precise, it started on the day we were discussing

26

some work of art and you uttered, quite seriously, the word *deconstruction*.

It wasn't so much the word deconstruction which upset me, it was the air of solemnity you imbued it with.

You said, humourlessly, unapologetically, without a trace of irony, the word *deconstruction*, you, my friend.

I wasn't sure how best to deal with the situation, so I made this throwaway remark, I said I think I must be getting intolerant in my old age, and you answered, who do you think you are? What makes you so high and mighty? . . .

What gives you the right to set yourself apart, Serge answered in the bloodiest possible way. And quite unexpectedly.

You're just Marc, what makes you think you're so special?

That day, I should have punched him in the mouth.

And when he was lying there on the ground, half-dead, I should have said to him, you're supposed to be my friend, what sort of a friend are you, Serge, if you don't think your friends are special?

At Serge's.
Marc and Serge, as we left them.

Marc Lyonnaise, did you say? Bit heavy, isn't it? Bit fatty, all those sausages . . . what do you think?

The doorbell rings.

Serge Twelve minutes past eight.

Serge goes to open the door to Yvan. Yvan walks into the room, already talking.

Yvan So, a crisis, insoluble problem, major crisis, both step-mothers want their names on the wedding invitation.

Catherine adores her step-mother, who more or less brought her up, she wants her name on the invitation, she wants it and her step-mother is not anticipating, which is understandable, since the mother is dead, not appearing next to Catherine's father, whereas my step-mother, whom I detest, it's out of the question her name should appear on the invitation, but my father won't have his name on it if hers isn't, unless Catherine's step-mother's is left off, which is completely unacceptable, I suggested none of the parents' names should be on it, after all we're not adolescents, we can announce our wedding and invite people ourselves, so Catherine screamed her head off, arguing that would be a slap in the face for her parents who were paying through the nose for the reception, and particularly for her step-mother, who's gone to so much trouble when she isn't even her daughter and I finally let myself be persuaded, totally against my better judgement, because she wore me down, I finally agreed that my step-mother, whom I detest, who's a complete bitch, will have her name on the invitation, so I telephoned my mother to warn her, mother, I said, I've done everything I can to avoid this, but we have absolutely no choice, Yvonne's name has to be on the invitation, she said, if Yvonne's name is on the invitation, take mine off it, mother, I said, please, I beg you, don't make things even more difficult, and she said, how dare you suggest my name is left to float around the card on its own, as if I was some aban-doned woman, below Yvonne, who'll be clamped on to your father's surname, like a limpet, I said to her, mother, I have friends waiting for me, I'm going to hang up and we'll discuss all this tomorrow after a good night's sleep, she said, why is it I'm always an afterthought, what are you talking about, mother, you're not always an after-thought, of course I am and when you say don't make things even more difficult, what you mean is, everything's already been decided, everything's been organized with-

28

out me, everything's been cooked up behind my back, good old Huguette, she'll agree to anything and all this, she said – to put the old tin lid on it – in aid of an event, the importance of which I'm having some trouble grasping, mother, I have friends waiting for me, that's right, there's always something better to do, anything's more important than I am, good-bye and she hung up, Catherine, who was next to me, but who hadn't heard her side of the conversation, said, what did she say, I said, she doesn't want her name on the invitation with Yvonne, which is understandable, I'm not talking about that, what was it she said about the wedding, nothing, you're lying, I'm not, Cathy, I promise you, she just doesn't want her name on the invitation with Yvonne, call her back and tell her when your son's getting married, you rise above your vanity, you could say the same thing to your stepmother, that's got nothing to do with it, Catherine shouted, it's me, I'm the one who's insisting her name's on it, it's not her, poor thing, she's tact personified, if she had any idea of the problem this is causing, she'd be down on her knees, begging for her name to be taken off the invitation, now call your mother, so I called her again, by now I'm in shreds, Catherine's listening on the extension, Yvan, my mother says, up to now you've conducted your affairs in the most chaotic way imaginable and just because, out of the blue, you've decided to embark on matrimony, I find myself obliged to spend all afternoon and evening with your father, a man I haven't seen for seventeen years and to whom I was not expecting to have to reveal my hip-size and my puffy cheeks, not to mention Yvonne who incidentally, I may tell you, according to Félix Perolari, has now taken up bridge – my mother also plays bridge – I can see none of this can be helped, but on the invitation, the one item everyone is going to receive and examine, I insist on making a solo appearance, Catherine, listening on the extension, shakes her head and screws up her face in disgust, mother, I say, why are you so selfish, I'm not selfish, I'm not selfish, Yvan, you're not going to start as well, you're not going to be like Mme Roméro this morning and tell me I have a heart of stone, that everybody in our family has a heart of stone, that's what Mme Roméro said this morning when I refused to raise her wages – she's gone completely mad, by the way – to sixty francs an hour tax-free, she had the gall to say everyone in the family had a heart of stone, when she knows very well about poor André's pacemaker, you haven't even bothered to drop him a line, yes, that's right, very funny, everything's a joke to you, it's not me who's the selfish one, Yvan, you've still got a lot to learn about life, off you go, my boy, go on, go on, go and see your precious friends . . .

Silence.

Serge Then what? . . .

Yvan Then nothing. Nothing's been resolved. I hung up. Mini-drama with Catherine. Cut short, because I was late.

Marc Why do you let yourself be buggered around by all these women?

Yvan Why do I let myself be buggered around, I don't know! They're all insane.

Serge You've lost weight.

Yvan Of course I have. Half a stone. Purely through stress.

Marc Read Seneca . . .

Yvan *De Vita Beata*, just what I need!
  What's he suggest?

Marc It's a masterpiece.

Yvan Oh?

Serge He hasn't read it.

Yvan Oh.

Marc No, but Serge just told me it was a masterpiece.

Serge I said it was a masterpiece because it is a masterpiece.

Marc Quite.

Serge It is a masterpiece.

Marc Why are you getting annoyed?

Serge You seem to be insinuating I use the word masterpiece at the slightest excuse.

Marc Not at all . . .

Serge You said the word in a kind of sarcastic way . . .

Marc Not at all!

Serge Yes, yes, the word masterpiece in a kind of . . .

Marc Is he crazy? Not at all! . . . However, when you used the word, you qualified it by saying 'incredibly modern'.

Serge Yes. So?

Marc You said 'incredibly modern', as if modern was the highest compliment you could give. As if, when describing something, you couldn't think of anything more admirable, more profoundly admirable, than modern.

Serge So?

Marc So nothing.
  And please note I made no mention of the word incredibly . . . Incredibly modern!

Serge You're really needling me today.

Marc No, I'm not . . .

31

Yvan You're not going to quarrel all evening, that would just about finish me!

Serge You don't think it's extraordinary that a man who wrote nearly two thousand years ago should still be bang up to date?

Marc No. Of course not. That's the definition of a classic.

Serge You're just playing with words.

Yvan So, what are we going to do? I suppose the cinema's up the spout, sorry. Shall we eat?

Marc Serge tells me you're very taken with his painting.

Yvan Yes . . . I am quite . . . taken with it, yes . . .
    You're not, I gather.

Marc No.
    Let's go and eat. Serge knows a tasty spot. Lyonnaise.

Serge You think the food's too fatty.

Marc I think the food's a bit on the fatty side, but I don't mind giving it a whirl.

Serge No, if you think the food's too fatty, we'll find somewhere else.

Marc No, I don't mind giving it a whirl.

Serge We'll go to the restaurant if you think you'll like it. If not, we won't.
    (*to Yvan*) You like Lyonnaise food?

Yvan I'll do whatever you like.

Marc He'll do whatever you like. Whatever you like, he'll always do.

Yvan What's the matter with you? You're both behaving very strangely.

Serge He's right, you might once in a while have an opinion of your own.

Yvan Listen, if you think you're going to use me as a coconut shy, I'm out of here! I've put up with enough today.

Marc Where's your sense of humour, Yvan?

Yvan What?

Marc Where's your sense of humour, old chap?

Yvan Where's my sense of humour? I don't see anything to laugh at. Where's my sense of humour, are you trying to be funny?

Marc I think recently you've somewhat lost your sense of humour. You want to watch out, believe me!

Yvan What's the matter with you?

Marc Don't you think recently I've also somewhat lost my sense of humour?

Yvan Oh, I see!

Serge All right, that's enough, let's make a decision. Tell you the truth, I'm not even hungry.

Yvan You're both really sinister this evening.

Serge You want my opinion about your women problems?

Yvan Go on.

Serge In my view, the most hysterical of them all is Catherine. By far.

Marc No question.

Serge And if you're already letting yourself be buggered around by her, you're in for a hideous future.

Yvan What can I do?

Marc Cancel it.

Yvan Cancel the wedding?

Serge He's right.

Yvan But I can't, are you crazy?

Marc Why not?

Yvan Well, because I can't, that's all! It's all arranged. I've only been working at the stationery business for a month . . .

Marc What's that got to do with it?

Yvan It's her uncle's stationery business, he had absolutely no need to take on anyone, least of all someone who's only ever worked in textiles.

Serge You must do what you like. I've told you what I think.

Yvan I'm sorry, Serge, I don't mean to be rude, but you're not necessarily the person I'd come to for matrimonial advice. You can't claim to have been a great success in that field . . .

Serge Precisely.

Yvan I can't back out of the wedding. I know Catherine is hysterical but she has her good points. There are certain crucial qualities you need when you're marrying someone like me . . . (*He indicates the Antrios.*) Where are you going to put it?

Serge I don't know yet.

Yvan Why don't you put it there?

Serge Because there, it'd be wiped out by the sunlight.

Yvan Oh, yes.

I thought of you today at the shop, we ran off five hundred posters by this bloke who paints white flowers, totally white, on a white background.

Serge The Antrios is not white.

Yvan No, of course not. I was just saying.

Marc You think this painting is not white, Yvan?

Yvan Not entirely, no . . .

Marc Ah. Then what colour is it?

Yvan Various colours . . . There's yellow, there's grey, some slightly ochrish lines.

Marc And you're moved by these colours?

Yvan Yes . . . I'm moved by these colours.

Marc You have no substance, Yvan. You're flabby, you're an amoeba.

Serge Why are you attacking Yvan like this?

Marc Because he's a little arse-licker, he's obsequious, dazzled by money, dazzled by what he believes to be culture, and as you know culture is something I absolutely piss on.

Brief silence.

Serge . . . What's got into you?

Marc (*to Yvan*) How could you, Yvan? . . . And in front of me. In front of me, Yvan.

Yvan What d'you mean, in front of you? . . . What d'you mean, in front of you?

I find these colours touching. Yes. If it's all the same to you.

Stop wanting to control everything.

Marc How could you say, in front of me, that you find these colours touching?

Yvan Because it's the truth.

Marc The truth? You find these colours touching?

Yvan Yes. I find these colours touching.

Marc You find these colours touching, Yvan?!

Serge He finds these colours touching! He's perfectly entitled to!

Marc No, he's not entitled to.

Serge What do you mean, he's not entitled to?

Marc He's not entitled to.

Yvan I'm not entitled to? . . .

Marc No.

Serge Why is he not entitled to? I don't think you're very well, perhaps you ought to go and see someone.

Marc He's not entitled to say he finds these colours touching, because he doesn't.

Yvan I don't find these colours touching?

Marc There are no colours. You can't see them. And you don't find them touching.

Yvan Speak for yourself!

Marc This is really demeaning, Yvan! . . .

Serge Who do you think you are, Marc? . . .
   Who are you to legislate? You don't like anything, you despise everyone. You take pride in not being a man of your time . . .

Marc What's that supposed to mean, a man of my time?

Yvan Right. I'm off.

Serge Where are you going?

Yvan I'm off. I don't see why I have to put up with your tantrums.

Serge Don't go! You're not going to start taking offence, are you? . . . If you go, you're giving in to him.

Yvan stands there, hesitating, caught between two possibilities.

A man of his time is a man who lives in his own time.

Marc Balls. How can a man live in any other time but his own? Answer me that.

Serge A man of his time is someone of whom it can be said in twenty years' or in a hundred years' time, he was representative of his era.

Marc Hm.
To what end?

Serge What do you mean, to what end?

Marc What use is it to me if one day somebody says, I was representative of my era?

Serge Listen, old fruit, we're not talking about you, if you can imagine such a thing! We don't give a fuck about you! A man of his time, I'm trying to explain to you, like most people you admire, is someone who makes some contribution to the human race . . . A man of his time doesn't assume the history of Art has come to an end with a pseudo-Flemish view of Cavaillon . . .

Marc Carcassonne.

Serge Same thing. A man of his time plays his part in the fundamental dynamic of evolution . . .

Marc And that's a good thing, in your view.

Serge It's not good or bad, why do you always have to moralize, it's just the way things are.

Marc And you, for example, you play your part in the fundamental dynamic of evolution.

Serge I do.

Marc What about Yvan? . . .

Yvan Surely not. What sort of part can an amoeba play?

Serge In his way, Yvan is a man of his time.

Marc How can you tell? Not from that daub hanging over his mantelpiece!

Yvan That is not a daub!

Serge It is a daub.

Yvan It is not!

Serge What's the difference? Yvan represents a certain way of life, a way of thinking which is completely modern. And so do you. I'm sorry, but you're a typical man of your time. And in fact, the harder you try not to be, the more you are.

Marc Well, that's all right then. So what's the problem?

Serge There's no problem, except for you, because you take pride in your desire to shut yourself off from humanity. And you'll never manage it. It's like you're in a quicksand, the more you struggle to get out of it, the deeper you sink. Now apologize to Yvan.

Marc Yvan is a coward.

> *At this point, Yvan makes his decision, and exits in a rush.*
> *Slight pause.*

Serge Well done.

Silence.

Marc It wasn't a good idea to meet this evening . . . was it? . . . I'd better go as well . . .

Serge Maybe . . .

Marc Right.

Serge You're the coward . . . attacking someone who's incapable of defending himself . . . as you well know.

Marc You're right . . . you're right and when you put it like that, it makes me feel even worse . . . the thing is, all of a sudden, I can't understand, I have no idea what Yvan and I have in common . . . I have no idea what my relationship with him consists of.

Serge Yvan's always been as he is.

Marc No. He used to be eccentric, kind of absurd . . . he was always unstable, but his eccentricity was disarming . . .

Serge What about me?

Marc What about you?

Serge Have you any idea what you and I have in common? . . .

Marc That's a question that could take us down a very long road . . .

Serge Lead on.

Short silence.

Marc . . . I'm sorry I upset Yvan.

Serge Ah! At last you've said something approximately human . . . What makes it worse is that the daub he has

39

hanging over his mantelpiece was I'm afraid painted by his father.

Marc Was it? Shit.

Serge Yes . . .

Marc But you said . . .

Serge Yes, yes, but I remembered as soon as I'd said it.

Marc Oh, shit . . .

Serge Mm . . .

> *Slight pause.*
> *The doorbell rings. Serge goes to answer it. Yvan enters immediately, talking as he arrives, as before.*

Yvan Yvan returns! The lift was full, I plunged off down the stairs, clattering all the way down thinking, a coward, an amoeba, no substance, I thought I'll come back with a gun and blow his head off, then he'll see how flabby and obsequious I am, I got to the ground floor and I said to myself, listen, mate, you haven't been in therapy for six years to finish up shooting your best friend and you haven't been in therapy for six years without learning that some deep malaise must lie behind his insane aggression, so I relaunch myself, telling myself as I mount the penitential stair, this is a cry for help. I have to help Marc if it's the last thing I do . . . In fact the other day I discussed you both with Finkelzohn . . .

Serge You discussed us with Finkelzohn?

Yvan I discuss everything with Finkelzohn.

Serge And why exactly were you discussing us?

Marc I forbid you to discuss me with that arsehole.

Yvan You're in no position to forbid me anything.

Serge Why were you discussing us?

Yvan I knew your relationship was under strain and I wanted Finkelzohn to explain . . .

Serge And what did the bastard say?

Yvan He said something rather amusing . . .

Marc They're allowed to give their opinions?

Yvan No, they never give their opinions, but this time he did give his opinion, he even made a gesture and he never makes a gesture, he's always rigid, I sometimes say to him, for God's sake, move about a bit! . . .

Serge All right, what did he say?

Marc Who gives a fuck what he said?

Serge What did he say?

Marc What possible interest could we have in what he said?

Serge I want to know what the bastard said, all right? Shit!

Yvan reaches into his jacket pocket.

Yvan You want to know? . . .

He fetches out a piece of folded paper.

Marc You took notes?

Yvan (*unfolding it*) I wrote it down because it was complicated . . . Shall I read it to you?

Serge Go on.

Yvan . . . 'If I'm who I am because I'm who I am and you're who you are because you're who you are, then I'm who I am and you're who you are. If, on the other hand, I'm who I am because you're who you are, and if you're

41

who you are because I'm who I am, then I'm not who I am and you're not who you are . . .'

You see why I had to write it down.

Short silence.

Marc How much do you pay this man?

Yvan Four hundred francs a session, twice a week.

Marc Great.

Serge And in cash. I found something out, they don't allow you to pay by cheque. Freud said you have to feel the banknotes as they slip through your fingers.

Marc What a lucky man you are, to be getting the benefit of this fellow's experience.

Serge Absolutely! . . . We'd really appreciate it if you'd copy that out for us.

Marc Yes. It's bound to come in handy.

Yvan carefully refolds the piece of paper.

Yvan You're wrong. It's very profound.

Marc If it's because of him you've come back to turn the other cheek, you should be grateful to him. He's turned you into a pudding, but you're happy, that's all that counts.

Yvan (*to Serge*) And all this because he doesn't want to believe I like your Antrios.

Serge I don't give a fuck what you think of it. Either of you.

Yvan The more I see it, the more I like it, honestly.

Serge Let's stop talking about the painting, shall we; once and for all. I have no interest in discussing it further.

Marc Why are you so touchy?

42

Serge I am not touchy, Marc. You've told us what you think. Fine. The subject is closed.

Marc You're getting upset.

Serge I am not getting upset. I'm exhausted.

Marc See, if you're touchy about it, it means you're too caught up in other people's opinions . . .

Serge I'm exhausted, Marc. This is completely pointless . . . To tell you the truth, I'm quite close to getting bored with the pair of you.

Yvan Let's go and eat.

Serge You go, why don't you go off together?

Yvan No! It's so rare the three of us are together.

Serge Just as well, by the look of it.

Yvan I don't understand what's going on. Can't we just calm down? There's no reason to insult each other, especially over a painting.

Serge You realize all this 'calm down' and behaving like the vicar is just adding fuel to the fire! Is this something new?

Yvan I will not be undermined.

Marc This is most impressive. Perhaps I should go to Finkelzohn! . . .

Yvan You can't. There are no vacancies.
    What's that you're eating?

Marc Gelsemium.

Yvan I've given in to the logic of events, marriage, children, death. Stationery. What can go wrong?

Moved by a sudden impulse, Serge picks up the Antrios

43

and takes it back where he found it, in the next room.
He returns immediately.

Marc We're not worthy to look at it . . .

Serge Exactly.

Marc Or are you afraid, if it stays in my presence, you'll finish up looking at it through my eyes? . . .

Serge No. You know what Paul Valéry says? And I'd go quite a bit further.

Marc I don't give a fuck what Paul Valéry says.

Serge You've gone off Paul Valéry?

Marc Don't quote Paul Valéry at me.

Serge But you used to love Paul Valéry.

Marc I don't give a fuck what Paul Valéry says.

Serge But I discovered him through you. You're the one who put me on to Paul Valéry.

Marc Don't quote Paul Valéry at me, I don't give a fuck what Paul Valéry says.

Serge What do you give a fuck about?

Marc I give a fuck about you buying that painting.
    I give a fuck about you spending two hundred grand on that piece of shit.

Yvan Don't start again, Marc!

Serge I'm going to tell you what I give a fuck about – since everyone is coming clean – I give a fuck about your sniggering and insinuations, your suggestion that I also think this picture is a grotesque joke. You've denied that I could feel a genuine attachment to it. You've tried to set up some kind of loathsome complicity between us. And

44

that's what's made me feel, Marc, to repeat your expression, that we have less and less in common recently, your perpetual display of suspicion.

Marc It's true I can't imagine you genuinely loving that painting.

Yvan But why?

Marc Because I love Serge and I can't love the Serge who's capable of buying that painting.

Serge Why do you say, buying, why don't you say, loving?

Marc Because I can't say loving, I can't believe loving.

Serge So why would I buy it, if I didn't love it?

Marc That's the nub of the question.

Serge (*to Yvan*) See how smug he is! All I'm doing is teasing him, and his answer is this serenely pompous heavy hint! . . . (*to Marc*) And it never crossed your mind for a second, however improbable it might seem, that I might really love it and that your vicious, inflexible opinions and your disgusting assumption of complicity might be hurtful to me?

Marc No.

Serge When you asked me what I thought of Paula – a girl who once spent an entire dinner party maintaining Elhers Danlos's syndrome could be cured homeopathically – did I say I found her ugly, repellent and charmless? I could have done.

Marc Is that what you think of Paula?

Serge What's your theory?

Yvan No, of course he doesn't think that! You couldn't possibly think that of Paula!

Marc Answer me.

Serge You see the effect you can have!

Marc Do you think what you just said about Paula?

Serge Worse, actually.

Yvan No!

Marc Worse, Serge? Worse than repellent? Will you explain how someone can be worse than repellent?

Serge Aha! When it's something that concerns you personally, I see words can bite a little deeper! . . .

Marc Serge, will you explain how someone can be worse than repellent . . .

Serge No need to take that frosty tone. Perhaps it's – let me try and answer you – perhaps it's the way she waves away cigarette smoke.

Marc The way she waves away cigarette smoke . . .

Serge Yes. The way she waves away cigarette smoke. What appears to you a gesture of no significance, what you think of as a harmless gesture is in fact the opposite, and the way she waves away cigarette smoke sits right at the heart of her repellentness.

Marc You're speaking to me of Paula, the woman who shares my life, in these intolerable terms, because you disapprove of her method of waving away cigarette smoke? . . .

Serge That's right. Her method of waving away cigarette smoke condemns her out of hand.

Marc Serge, before I completely lose control, you'd better explain yourself. This is very serious, what you're doing.

Serge A normal woman would say, I'm sorry, I find the

smoke a bit uncomfortable, would you mind moving your ashtray, but not her, she doesn't deign to speak, she describes her contempt in the air with this calculated gesture, wearily malicious, this hand movement she imagines is imperceptible, the implication of which is to say, go on, smoke, smoke, it's pathetic but what's the point of calling attention to it, which means you can't tell if it's you or your cigarette that's getting up her nose.

Yvan You're exaggerating!

Serge You notice he doesn't say I'm wrong, he says I'm exaggerating, but he doesn't say I'm wrong. Her method of waving away cigarette smoke reveals a cold, condescending and narrow-minded nature. Just what you're in the process of acquiring yourself. It's a shame, Marc, it's a real shame you've taken up with such a life-denying woman . . .

Yvan Paula is not life-denying! . . .

Marc Take back everything you've just said, Serge.

Serge No.

Yvan Yes, you must!

Marc Take back what you've just said . . .

Yvan Take it back, take it back! This is ridiculous!

Marc Serge, for the last time, I demand you take back what you've just said.

Serge In my view, the two of you are an aberration. A pair of fossils.

Marc throws himself at Serge. Yvan rushes forward to get between them.

Marc (*to Yvan*) Get off! . . .

47

Serge (*to Yvan*) Mind your own business! . . .

*A kind of bizarre struggle ensues, very short, which
ends with a blow mistakenly landing on Yvan.*

Yvan Oh, shit! . . . Oh, shit! . . .

Serge Show me, show me . . .

Yvan is groaning. More than is necessary, it would seem.

Come on, show me! . . . That's all right . . . it's nothing
. . . Wait a minute . . .

He goes out and comes back with a compress.

There you are, hold that on it for a while.

Yvan . . . You're complete freaks, both of you. Two normal men gone completely insane!

Serge Don't get excited.

Yvan That really hurt! . . . If I find out you've burst my
eardrum! . . .

Serge Of course not.

Yvan How do you know? You're not ear, nose and
throat! . . . Two old friends, educated people! . . .

Serge Go on, calm down.

Yvan You can't demolish someone because you don't like
her method of waving away cigarette smoke! . . .

Serge Yes, you can.

Yvan But it doesn't make any sense!

Serge What do you know about sense?

Yvan That's right, attack me, keep attacking me! . . . I
could be haemorrhaging internally, I've just seen a mouse
running past! . . .

Serge It's a rat.

Yvan A rat?

Serge He comes and goes.

Yvan You have a rat?!

Serge Don't take the compress away, leave it where it is.

Yvan What's the matter with you? . . . What's happened between you? Something must have happened for you to go this demented.

Serge I've bought a work of art which makes Marc uncomfortable.

Yvan You're starting again! . . . You're in a downward spiral, both of you, you can't stop yourselves . . . It's like me and Yvonne. The most pathological relationship you can imagine!

Serge Who's Yvonne?

Yvan My step-mother!

Serge It's a long time since you mentioned her.

Brief silence.

Marc Why didn't you tell me right away what you thought about Paula?

Serge I didn't want to upset you.

Marc No, no, no . . .

Serge What do you mean, no, no, no? . . .

Marc No.
   When I asked you what you thought of Paula, what you said was: she's a perfect match for you.

Serge Yes . . .

49

Marc Which sounded quite positive, coming from you.

Serge Sure . . . .

Marc Given the state you were in at the time.

Serge All right, what are you trying to prove?

Marc But today, your assessment of Paula, or in other words me, is far harsher.

Serge . . . I don't understand.

Marc Of course you understand.

Serge I don't.

Marc Since I can no longer support you in your frenzied, though recent, craving for novelty, I've become 'condescending', 'narrow-minded' . . . 'fossilized' . . .

Yvan I'm in agony! It's like a corkscrew drilling through my brain!

Serge Have a drop of brandy.

Yvan What do you think? . . . If something's shaken loose in my brain, don't you think alcohol's a bit of a risk?

Serge Would you like an aspirin?

Yvan I'm not sure aspirin agrees with me . . .

Serge Then what the hell do you want?

Yvan Don't worry about me. Carry on with your preposterous conversation, don't pay any attention to me.

Marc Easier said than done.

Yvan You might squeeze out a drop of compassion. But no.

Serge I don't mind your spending time with Paula. I don't resent you being with Paula.

Marc You've no reason to resent it.

Serge But you . . . you resent me . . . well, I was about to say, for being with the Antrios!

Marc Yes!

Serge I'm missing something here.

Marc I didn't replace you with Paula.

Serge Are you saying, I replaced you with the Antrios?

Marc Yes.

Serge . . . I replaced you with the Antrios?

Marc Yes. With the Antrios . . . and all it implies.

Serge (*to Yvan*) Do you understand what he's talking about?

Yvan I couldn't care less, you're both insane.

Marc In my time, you'd never have bought that picture.

Serge What's that supposed to mean, in your time?

Marc The time you made a distinction between me and other people, when you judged things by my standards.

Serge Was there such a time?

Marc That's just cruel. And petty.

Serge No, I assure you, I'm staggered.

Marc And if Yvan hadn't turned into such a sponge, he'd back me up.

Yvan Go on, that's right, I've told you, it's water off a duck's back.

Marc (*to Serge*) There was a time you were proud to be my friend . . . You congratulated yourself on my peculiarity, on my taste for standing apart. You enjoyed exhibiting me untamed to your circle, you, whose life was so normal. I was your alibi. But . . . eventually, I suppose, that sort of affection dries up . . . Belatedly, you claim your independence.

Serge 'Belatedly' is nice.

Marc But I detest your independence. Its violence. You've abandoned me. I've been betrayed. As far as I'm concerned, you're a traitor.

Silence.

Serge (*to Yvan*) . . . If I understand correctly, he was my mentor! . . .

Yvan doesn't respond. Marc stares at him contemptuously. Slight pause.

. . . And if I loved you as my mentor . . . what was the nature of your feelings?

Marc You can guess.

Serge Yes, yes, but I want to hear you say it.

Marc . . . I enjoyed your admiration. I was flattered. I was always grateful to you for thinking of me as a man apart. I even thought being a man apart was a somehow superior condition, until one day you pointed out to me that it wasn't.

Serge This is very alarming.

Marc It's the truth.

Serge What a disaster . . .!

Marc Yes, what a disaster!

Serge What a disaster!

Marc Especially for me . . . Whereas you've found a new family. Your penchant for idolatry has unearthed new objects of worship. The Artist! . . . *Deconstruction*!

Short silence.

Yvan What is deconstruction? . . .

Marc You don't know about deconstruction? . . . Ask Serge, he's very much on top of the subject . . . (*to Serge*) To convince me some ridiculous artwork is comprehensible, you pick a phrase from *Builders' Weekly* . . . Oh, you're smiling! You see, when you smile like that, I think there's still some hope, like an idiot . . .

Yvan Why don't you make up? And let's spend an enjoyable evening, all this is ludicrous!

Marc . . . It's my fault. We haven't seen much of one another recently. I've been away and you started mixing with the great and the good . . . the Ropses . . . the Desprez-Couderts . . . that dentist, Guy Hallié . . . he's the one who . . .

Serge No, no, no, no, not at all, he's from another world, he only likes conceptual Art . . .

Marc It's all the same thing.

Serge No, it's not all the same thing.

Marc You see, more evidence of how I let you slip away . . . now when we talk we can't even make ourselves understood.

Serge I had no idea whatsoever – really, it's come as a complete surprise – the extent to which I was under your influence and in your control.

Marc Not in my control, as it turns out . . . You should never leave your friends unchaperoned. Your friends need to be chaperoned, otherwise they'll get away . . .

Look at poor Yvan, whose chaotic behaviour used to delight us, we've allowed him to become this timid stationer . . . Practically married . . . He brought us his originality and now he's making every effort to piss it away.

Serge Us! He brought us! Do you realize what you're saying? Everything has to revolve around you! Why can't you learn to love people for themselves, Marc?

Marc What does that mean, for themselves?

Serge For what they are.

Marc But what are they?! What are they?! . . .
Apart from my faith in them? . . .
I'm desperate to find a friend who has some kind of prior existence. So far, I've had no luck. I've had to mould you . . . But you see, it never works. There comes a day when your creature has dinner with the Desprez-Couderts and, to confirm his new status, goes off and buys a white painting.

Silence.

Serge So here we are at the end of a fifteen-year friendship . . .

Marc Yes . . .

Yvan Pathetic . . .

Marc You see, if we'd only managed to have a normal discussion, that is, if I'd have been able to put my point of view without losing my temper . . .

Serge Well? . . .

Marc Nothing . . .

Serge Yes. Go on. Why can't we exchange one single dispassionate word?

Marc . . . I don't believe in the values which dominate contemporary Art. The rule of novelty. The rule of surprise.

Surprise is dead meat, Serge. No sooner conceived than dead.

Serge All right. So?

Marc That's all.

Except that my appeal to you has always been my surprise value.

Serge What are you talking about?

Marc A surprise which has lasted quite some time, I'll admit.

Yvan Finkelzohn is a genius.

I told you he'd understood the whole thing!

Marc I'd prefer it if you stopped refereeing, Yvan, and stopped imagining you're not fully implicated in this conversation.

Yvan You want to implicate me, I refuse, what's it to do with me? I've already got a burst eardrum, you work things out for yourselves!

Marc Perhaps he does have a burst eardrum. I hit him very hard.

Serge sniggers.

Serge Please, stop boasting.

Marc See, Yvan, what I can't bear about you at the moment – quite apart from what I've already told you – is your urge to put Serge and me on the same level. You would like us to be equal. To indulge your cowardice. Talking on an equal footing, equal the way you thought of us when we were friends. But we never were equal, Yvan. You have to choose.

Yvan I have chosen.

Marc Excellent.

Serge I don't need a supporter.

Marc You're not going to turn the poor boy down?

Yvan Why do we see each other, if we hate each other? It's obvious we do hate each other! Or rather, I don't hate you, but you hate each other! And you hate me! So why do we see each other? . . . I was looking forward to a relaxing evening after a ridiculously fraught week, meeting my two best friends, going to the cinema, having a laugh, getting away from all these dramas . . .

Serge Are you aware that you've talked about nothing but yourself?

Yvan Well, who are you talking about? Everybody talks about themselves!

Serge You fuck up our evening, you . . .

Yvan I fuck up your evening?! . . .

Serge Yes.

Yvan I fuck up your evening?! I?! I fuck up your evening?!

Marc All right, don't get excited!

Yvan You're saying it's me who's fucked up your evening?! . . .

Serge How many more times are you going to say it?

Yvan Just answer the question, are you saying it's me who's fucked up your evening?! . . .

Marc You arrive three-quarters of an hour late, you don't apologize, you deluge us with your domestic woes . . .

Serge And your inertia, your sheer neutral spectator's inertia has lured Marc and me into the worst excesses.

Yvan You as well! You're starting as well?

Serge Yes, because on this subject I'm entirely in agreement with him. You create the conditions of conflict.

Marc You've been piping up with this finicky, subservient voice of reason ever since you arrived, it's intolerable.

Yvan You know I could burst into tears . . . I could start crying right now . . . I'm very close to tears.

Marc Cry.

Serge Cry.

Yvan Cry! You're telling me to cry!

Marc You've every reason to cry, you're marrying a gorgon, you're losing your two best friends . . .

Yvan That's it then, is it, it's all over!

Marc You said it yourself, what's the point of seeing each other, if we hate each other?

Yvan What about my wedding?! You're my witnesses, remember?

Serge Find someone else.

Yvan I can't! You're on the invitation!

Marc You can choose someone else at the last minute.

Yvan You're not allowed to!

Serge Of course you are!

Yvan You're not! . . .

Marc Don't panic, we'll come.

Serge But what you ought to do is cancel the wedding.

Marc He's right.

Yvan Oh, shit! What have I ever done to you? Shit!

He bursts into tears.
Time passes.

It's brutal what you're doing! You could have had your fight after the 12th, but no, you're determined to ruin my wedding, a wedding which is already a catastrophe, which has made me lose half a stone and now you're completely buggering it up! The only two people whose presence guaranteed some spark of satisfaction are determined to destroy one another, just my luck! . . . (*to Marc*) You think I like packs of filofax paper or rolls of sellotape, you think any normal man wakes up one day desperate to sell expandable document wallets? . . . What am I supposed to do? I pissed around for forty years, I made you laugh, oh, yes, wonderful, I made all my friends laugh their heads off playing the fool, but come the evening, who was left solitary as a rat? Who crawled back into his hole every evening all on his own? This buffoon, dying of loneliness, who'd switch on anything that talks and who does he find on the answering machine? His mother. His mother. And his mother.

A short silence.

Marc Don't get yourself in such a state.

Yvan Don't get yourself in such a state! Who got me in this state in the first place? Look at me – I don't have your refined sensibilities. I'm a lightweight. I have no opinions.

Marc Calm down . . .

Yvan Don't tell me to calm down! What possible reason do I have to calm down, are you trying to drive me demented, telling me to calm down? Calm down's the worst thing you can say to someone who's lost his calm! I'm not like you, I don't want to be an authority figure, I don't want to be a point of reference, I don't want to be self-sufficient, I just want to be your friend Yvan the joker! Yvan the joker!

Silence.

Serge Could we try to steer clear of pathos? . . .

Yvan I've finished.
Haven't you got any nibbles? Anything, just to stop from passing out.

Serge I have some olives.

Yvan Hand them over.

Serge reaches for a little bowl of olives and hands it to him.

Serge (*to Marc*) Want some?

Marc nods. Yvan hands him the bowl. They eat olives.

Yvan Is there somewhere to put the . . .

Serge Yes.

He fetches a saucer and puts it on the table.
Pause.

Yvan (*still eating olives*) . . . To think we've reached these extremes . . . Apocalypse because of a white square . . .

Serge It is not white.

Yvan A piece of white shit! . . .

He's seized by uncontrollable laughter.

That's what it is, a piece of white shit! . . . Let's face it, mate . . . What you've bought is insane! . . .

Marc laughs, caught up by Yvan's extravagance. Serge leaves the room. He returns immediately with the Antrios.

Serge Do you have one of your famous felt-tips? . . .

Yvan What for? . . . You're not going to draw on the painting.

Serge Do you or don't you?

Yvan Just a minute . . . (*He goes through the pockets of his jacket.*) Yes . . . A blue one . . .

Serge Give it to me.

Yvan hands the felt-tip to Serge.
  Serge takes the felt-tip, pulls the top off it, examines the tip for a moment, puts the top back on.
  He looks up at Marc and throws him the felt-tip. Marc catches it.
  Slight pause.

(*to Marc*) Go on.

Silence.

Go on!

Marc approaches the painting . . .
  He looks at Serge . . .
  Then he takes the top off the felt-tip.

Yvan You're not going to do it! . . .

Marc is looking at Serge.

Serge Come on.

Yvan You're raving mad, both of you!

Marc leans towards the painting.
  Under Yvan's horrified gaze, he draws the felt-tip

60

along one of the diagonal scars. Serge remains impassive.

Then, carefully, on this slope, Marc draws a little skier with a woolly hat.

When he's finished, he straightens up and contemplates his work.

Serge remains adamantine.

Yvan is as if turned to stone.

Silence.

Serge Well, I'm starving.
Shall we eat?

Marc tries a smile. He puts the top back on and playfully throws the pen to Yvan, who catches it.

At Serge's.

At the back, hanging on the wall, the Antrios. Standing in front of the canvas, Marc is holding a basin of water, into which Serge is dipping a little piece of cloth. Marc has rolled up his sleeves and Serge is wearing a little builder's apron which is too short for him. Round about are various cleaning products, bottles of white spirit and stain remover, rags and sponges. Moving very delicately, Serge puts the finishing touch to the cleaning of the painting.

The Antrios is as white as ever. Marc puts down the basin and looks at the painting. Serge turns to Yvan, who's sitting off to one side. Yvan nods approvingly. Serge steps back and contemplates the picture in his turn.

Silence.

Yvan *(as if alone, speaking in a slightly muffled voice)* . . .
The day after the wedding, at the Montparnasse cemetery, Catherine put her wedding bouquet and a little bag of sugared almonds on her mother's grave. I slipped away to cry behind a monument and in the evening, thinking

again about this touching tribute, I started silently sob-
bing in my bed. I absolutely must speak to Finkelzohn
about my tendency to cry, I cry all the time, it's not normal for someone my age. It started, or at least clearly
revealed itself at Serge's, the evening of the white painting.
After Serge, in an act of pure madness, had demonstrated
to Marc that he cared more about him than he did about
his painting, we went and had dinner, chez Emile. Over
dinner, Serge and Marc took the decision to try to rebuild
a relationship destroyed by word and deed. At a certain
moment, one of them used the expression 'trial period'
and I burst into tears.

This expression, 'trial period', applied to our friendship, set off in me an uncontrollable and ridiculous con-
vulsion.

In fact I can no longer bear any kind of rational argu-
ment, nothing formative in the world, nothing great or
beautiful in the world has ever been born of rational argu-
ment.

Pause.

*Serge dries his hands. He goes to empty the basin of
water then puts away all the cleaning products, until
there's no sign left of domestic activity. Once again he
looks at his painting. Then he turns and advances
towards the audience.*

Serge When Marc and I succeeded in obliterating the
skier, with the aid of Swiss soap with added ox gall, recommended by Paula, I looked at the Antrios and turned
to Marc:

'Did you know ink from felt-tips was washable?'

'No,' Marc said . . . 'No . . . did you?'

'No,' I said, very fast, lying. I came within an inch of
saying, yes, I did know. But how could I have launched
our trial period with such a disappointing admission? . . .
On the other hand, was it right to start with a lie? . . . A

lie! Let's be reasonable. Why am I so absurdly virtuous? Why does my relationship with Marc have to be so complicated? . . .

Gradually, the light begins to narrow down on the Antrios. Marc approaches the painting.

Marc Under the white clouds, the snow is falling.
   You can't see the white clouds, or the snow.
   Or the cold, or the white glow of the earth.
   A solitary man glides downhill on his skis.
   The snow is falling.
   It falls until the man disappears back into the landscape.
   My friend Serge, who's one of my oldest friends, has bought a painting.
   It's a canvas about five foot by four.
   It represents a man who moves across a space and disappears.